# CONTENTS

# WANT TO BE A WRITER?

**T**his book aims to give you the tools to write your own realistic fiction. Learn how to craft believable characters, perfect plots, and satisfying beginnings, middles and endings.

## Step-by-step instruction

The pages throughout the book include numbers providing step-by-step instructions or a series of options that will help you to master certain parts of the writing process. To create beginnings, middles and ends, for example, complete 17 simple steps.

## Chronological progress

You can follow your progress by using the bar located on the bottom of each page. The orange colour tells you how far along the story-writing process you have got. As the blocks are filled out, so your story will be gathering pace... Each section explains a key part of the writing process, teaching you how to get into the mindset of an author and learn all the necessary skills, from plot structure and viewpoints to adding belieavable dialogue. The process ends by looking at the next step – what do you want to do next after your story is finished.

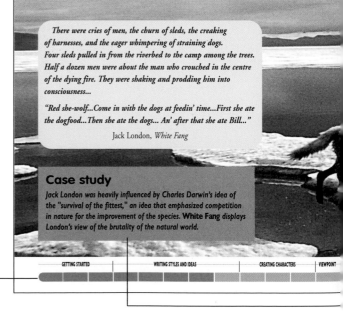

### 20 HOW TO CREATE A LANDSCAPE

**❶ Research a setting**

In realistic fiction, the setting will play a big part in how everyone behaves, be it a war zone or the city streets. To tell a convincing tale, you will need to understand how the setting operates.

**❷ Make the location thrilling**

Don't bore readers by describing absolutely everything about your physical location. But make sure you know how the location will influence the human story. This calls for research. Imagine you're doing a geography assignment; look for details on human settlement patterns, climate, natural history, communications or emergency services. Sketching setting details will help you to understand them better. Choose the most dramatic features to use in your story.

**❸ Add more action**

In Jack London's *White Fang*, he conjures the harshness of the terrain in this grizzly incident:

> There were cries of men, the churn of sleds, the creaking of harnesses, and the eager whimpering of straining dogs. Four sleds pulled in from the riverbed to the camp among the trees. Half a dozen men were about the man who crouched in the centre of the dying fire. They were shaking and prodding him into consciousness...
>
> "Red she-wolf...Come in with the dogs at feedin' time...First she ate the dogfood...Then she ate the dogs... An' after that she ate Bill..."
>
> Jack London, *White Fang*

**Case study**

Jack London was heavily influenced by Charles Darwin's idea of the "survival of the fittest," an idea that emphasized competition in nature for the improvement of the species. **White Fang** displays London's view of the brutality of the natural world.

GETTING STARTED | WRITING STYLES AND IDEAS | CREATING CHARACTERS | VIEWPOINT

# Box features

Appearing throughout the book, these four different colour-coded box types help you with the writing process by providing inspiration, examples from other books, background details and hints and tips.

## Now it's your turn

**A sense of place**
Go back to your 'chance concoctions' options (see page 18). Think about the 'character' and 'place' that you dealt from your cards. For ten minutes, write a scene that describes your chosen place from the character's point of view. Imagine they are upset (decide why first) and find ways to reflect this in your description. Take a break and then repeat the exercise, but this time write to reflect a positive feeling – joy, relief or hope.

### ⑭ Use the setting to reveal feelings
At the start of Sharon Creech's *Walk Two Moons*, Salamanca is shocked when her father insists they move from their Kentucky farm to live in a town. What does her description of her new home reveal about her feelings?

> *Tiny, squirt trees. Little birdhouses in a row – and one of those birdhouses was ours. No swimming hole, no barn, no cows, no chickens, no pigs...*
> *"Let's take a tour," my father said, rather too heartily.*
> *We walked through the tiny living room into the miniature kitchen and upstairs into...my pocket-sized bedroom...*
> Sharon Creech, *Walk Two Moons*

**TIPS AND TECHNIQUES**
*When setting any scene, think of ways to trigger the senses. How does it smell, feel, sound, taste and look from inside your own skin? Keep thinking too: how does it affect my characters and their actions?*

SYNOPSES & PLOTS | WINNING WORDS | SCINTILLATING SPEECH | HINTS & TIPS | FINISHING TOUCHES | WHAT NEXT!

## Now it's your turn boxes
These boxes provide a chance for you to put into practice what you have just been reading about. Simple, useful and fun exercises to help you build your writing skills.

## Quote boxes
Turn to these green boxes to find quotes taken from published realistic-fiction books by popular authors, from Jacqueline Wilson to Jack Gantos.

## Tips and techniques boxes
These boxes provide writing tips that will help you when you get stuck, or provided added inspiration to get to the next level.

## Case study boxes
These boxes provide history on famous realistic-fiction writers - what inspired them, how they started and more details.

# WHY DO WRITERS WRITE?

**E**very writer says the same: writing is hard work; you must stick at it through thick and thin, even when writing is the last thing you feel like doing. So if it's not easy, why do writers write? They write because they must. They write to tell a story that must be told. They write because they believe that nothing is more important than stories. They write because it's the thing they most want to do. Here is some advice from famous writers:

## Jack Gantos

Author Jack Gantos says that the biggest hurdle is getting started. He also says that writers of all ages have this problem because they think nothing interesting happens to them. He believes that keeping a diary is a good way for a fiction writer to start. Jack Gantos began his writing career with the *Rotten Ralph* picture books. These were inspired by the antics of his bad cat (left)!

## Jacqueline Wilson

Jacqueline has been a professional writer since she was 17, when she went to work for a teenage magazine called *Jackie*. But when she was nine, she wrote a story about a family with problems, and she has been writing stories like this ever since. She writes with an appealing mix of sorrow and humour. Her advice – *Keep a diary to get into an automatic daily writing habit.*

## Anne Fine

Her most famous book is *Madame Doubtfire*, which was made into a film. It deals with parental separation and divorce. Most of her stories explore serious family issues in a humorous way. Her advice? *Read, read, read,'* and *'Write the book you would most like to read.*

## Michael Morpurgo

To break writer's block, Michael Morpurgo says: *If you get stuck (and I do often) go for a long, long walk, tell yourself the story aloud.* He also says he gets his ideas from his memories and interests. He does a lot of historical research, too. He believes that every writer must find their own way of working, and that there is no right or wrong way. His advice is: *Tell it from the heart, as you feel your story, as you see it.*

## Judy Blume

This award-winning author (left) says that - *Ideas come from everywhere – memories of my own life, incidents in my children's lives, what I see and hear and read – and most of all, from my imagination.* She has used her own experiences in many of her books. Her own family life was a lot like the family in *Starring Sally J. Freedman As Herself.* Fudge in *Tales of a Fourth Grade Nothing* is based on her own son Larry when he was a toddler (although he did not swallow a turtle as Fudge does!).

# FIRST THINGS FIRST

**F**irst gather your writing materials and find your story-making place. Writers are lucky. They can write wherever they please, as long as they have pen and paper. A computer can make writing quicker, but is not essential.

## Gather your writing materials

The following materials will help you organise your thoughts as you learn your craft and do your research at the library or on the internet.

- A pocket notebook that you carry everywhere.
- Large spiral-bound notebooks and scrap paper.

- Pencils and pens with different coloured ink.
- Post-it notes for research ideas.
- Stick-on stars for highlighting stunning thoughts.
- Folders for storing up good story ideas.
- Dictionary, thesaurus and encyclopaedia.
- A camera to capture real people and places for your research.

## ❷ Create a writing place

Next you need to decide where your writing zone will be. Jacqueline Wilson writes on trains between schools visits. Judy Blume has a writing shack on an island. David Almond writes in a spare bedroom and on trains too. Your bedroom may be the best place, or the library where you can watch people while you work.

## ❸ Create a writing zone

• Play music that makes you feel calm and thoughtful;

• Make a collection of striking images of people and places;

• Have a hat or jacket that you only wear when you're writing;

• Choose some special objects to have around you while you work – a pen you use only for creative writing; a beautiful crystal to focus your thoughts; a snow dome (to shake up your ideas).

### TIPS AND TECHNIQUES

*Once you have found your writing place, the golden rule of becoming a real writer is: Go there as often as possible, and write something! This is calle the writers golden rule.*

## ❹ Get in training

Before you can write captivating stories, you must begin training as a writer. Learning to write when you don't feel at all inspired is an important part of becoming a writer. To create the writing habit, good writers do daily practice, just as a musician plays scales or an athlete does press-ups. However much you might not feel like writing, it is important to make it a regular habit.

## ❺ Keep going

The more you do exercises like these, the easier it will be to defeat the Story Saboteur – your internal critic who says your writing is useless. Try these storylines at practice time:

• *The day my house burned down and I became homeless.*
• *My most embarrassing experience.*
• *My best and worst birthdays.*

## Now it's your turn

### Unlock your imagination

Begin your practise with some timed brainstorming to shake up your creativity. Have pen and scrap paper ready. Sit in your writing zone, close your eyes and take four long, deep breaths. Then write the phrase 'Everything I've ever wanted to do' at the top of the paper. For two minutes write anything that comes into your head. Go, Go. GO! SPOUT like a fountain! Stop after two minutes. Hurray! You can write!

## TIPS AND TECHNIQUES

*Have a set time for your writing practice – ten minutes a day or an hour a week. Whatever you decide, make a date with your writing zone. Come winter heatwave or summer snow, don't be distracted.*

## 6 Reward yourself!

When you've finished, give yourself a gold star. You have unlocked your Long-lost Story Archive. The more you do this, the easier it will be to overcome the Story Executioner – your internal critic that always finds fault with your writing.

## Case study

*Louise Erdrich, author of* **The Birchbark House**, *wrote a lot as a child. Her father gave her a nickel for every story she wrote, and her mother made each story a wonderful cover. Louise Erdrich says:* **At an early age I felt myself to be a published author earning substantial royalties.**

### ❼ Read, read, read!

All good writing starts with lots of good reading. You might choose to read realistic fiction about what it feels like to have a mother with tattoos; bullying; or running away. See what grabs your imagination!

### ❽ Discover your tastes

Read as many different kinds of realistic fiction as you can. This will help you to decide the kinds of story you most want to write. Start an 'ideas' file.

### ❾ Look more deeply

Think carefully about the books you enjoy. Do you like the gritty drama of books such as Robert Cormier's *Heroes* and Alan Gibbons (right)' *The Edge*? Or do you prefer Paula Danziger's wry humour? Re-read one of your favourite books. Instead of losing yourself in it as the writer intended, imagine you are writing the story. Work out how the writer creates suspense, brings settings to life and makes the characters seem real.

### Now it's your turn

#### Making real life magic

Imagine you are in charge of organising a family festival – a birthday or a religious celebration. But you have no money to spend. Spend ten minutes describing what you will do to make it really special for everyone. Jot down your first thoughts.

## Case studies

Louisa May Alcott's **Little Women**, published in 1868, is based on her own impoverished family life. The book's straightforward style has made it a bestseller ever since. Charles Dickens knew all about hard times. His own father was sent to a debtor's prison and the writer used these experiences when he wrote **Little Dorrit**. After leaving school he worked for a law firm, recording court proceedings, and then as a parliamentary journalist. He had the best possible practice for becoming one of the world's greatest writers of realistic fiction.

## TIPS AND TECHNIQUES

The key to writing good realistic fiction is to tell a believable story from an unexpected angle. Think personal and look to the heart of things as you write.

# A WRITER'S VOICE

To be a good reader you need to read with attention. This will help you to discover your own writer's voice – a style of writing uniquely yours. But it will take time; writers go on developing their voices all their lives.

## Finding your voice

Once you start reading as a would-be writer, you will see that every writer has their own rhythm, style and range of vocabulary. For instance, *Because of Winn-Dixie* author Kate Di Camillo 'sounds' very different from *The Illustrated Mum* author Jacqueline Wilson.

## ❷ Experiment

For storytelling ideas, try reading other genres. Caroline Lawrence sets her detective stories in Ancient Rome. Legends might inspire you, too, as they did Kevin Crossley-Holland in the *Arthur* series.

### Now it's your turn

#### Personal experiences
Read the extracts opposite and copy out the one you like best. Does the piece remind you of something that happened to you? If it does, write down your own story. Try writing it in a humorous style, and then in a tragic or sarcastic one.

# WRITERS' VOICES

**Look at the words these authors use. Think about the rhythm and length of sentences. Which style do you prefer?**

## Dodie Smith

I Capture the Castle *begins with a most unusual opening:*

> *I write this sitting in the kitchen sink. That is, my feet are in it; the rest of me is on the draining-board, which I have padded with our dog's blanket and the tea-cosy. I can't say that I am really comfortable…but this is the only part of the kitchen where there is any daylight left. And I have found that sitting in a place that you have never sat before can be inspiring – I wrote my very best poem while sitting on the hen-house.*
>
> Dodie Smith, *I Capture the Castle*

## Charles Dickens

*In* Great Expectations, *escaped convict Magwitch ambushes the hero Pip:*

> *A man started up from among the graves at the side of the church porch.*
>
> *"Keep still you little devil, or I'll cut your throat!"*
>
> *A man who had been soaked in water, and smothered in mud, and lamed by stones, and cut by flints, and stung by nettles, and torn by briars; who limped, and shivered, and glared and growled; and whose teeth chattered in his head as he seized me by the chin.*
>
> Charles Dickens, *Great Expectations*

## Sharon Creech

*In* Heartbeat, *Annie tells the story of her life in poems:*

> *Sometimes when I am running a boy appears like my sideways shadow from the trees he emerges running falling into thump-thump steps beside me.*
>
> Sharon Creech, *Heartbeat*

### ❸ Where to start?

Stories rarely drop into writers' minds fully formed. They begin with one or two ideas, which the writer then must research and develop. But where do writers get their ideas from in the first place? There are many different sources out there.

### ❹ Use what you know

Many famous writers use their own life experiences to write their fiction. This is a good way to start. If you write about what you know and feel and have seen, you will have plenty of good raw materials for crafting believable settings and characters.

Your diary accounts will become your raw materials. They will have plenty of insights, but to make a good story with a believable hero out of them, you may have to exaggerate or alter events.

### ❺ Keep a diary

And before you say 'Nothing interesting ever happens to me!', remember your burning ambitions. If nothing happened today, write about your hopes and dreams.

Put a reminder in your diary – *Everything in my life is special in some way: I only have to look!*

### TIPS AND TECHNIQUES

*Say you want to turn the details of a school camping trip into a good story. First think who your main character will be. It could be the shy class weakling, Max. How does he stop being a victim and become a hero?*

## Now it's your turn

### And then what...?

Was Max, the main character from your camping story (see the Tips and Techniques opposite) ambushed by bullies and left dangling upside down from a tree? Finish the story in your next writing practice. Asking questions will help you shape the plot. What if your hero decided to fight back? How would he do it? What are the bullies' weak points?

## ❻ Good topics

Winning a match, getting bad grades, training for a team, learning new skills, a family party, a bad day at school, a school trip, embarrassing moments, a camping expedition, foreign travel, an argument with your best friend, a hospital visit, cleaning out your granny's attic, the view from your window, an issue you care about deeply.

### TIPS AND TECHNIQUES

*Read some real-life diaries.* **Thura's Diary** *is the account of a young girl's life in war-torn Baghdad by Thura Al-Windawi. Also try fictional diary stories like Sharon Creech's* **Absolutely Normal Chaos** *or Sue Townsend's* **The Secret Diary of Adrian Mole, aged 13 ¾.**

## ❼ Do your research

Writing from first-hand experience is hard to beat, but if you want to write about someone whose life you've only glimpsed, some serious research is called for to make your story believable. Suppose you want to write a story about a young film or rock star. Begin by reading about as many real child stars as possible – Britney Spears or Macaulay Culkin (right), for example.

## ❽ Gather information

Collect articles from celebrity magazines and newspapers. Look at stars' official sites on the Internet. Make notes on what they say about themselves and how they live. Write down the actual words they use. Research stars from past eras too, such as Shirley Temple and Judy Garland.

## TIPS AND TECHNIQUES

*Start a newspaper-cuttings file of intriguing stories. Collect the most dramatic stories (such as kids who have won despite all the odds) and cut out photos of interesting characters.*

## ❾ Build a fictional star's profile

Build up a celebrity profile based on several stars' lives. If you do your research well, you will find all the real-life conflict and drama you need to make an interesting story.

## Now it's your turn

### A perfect recipe?

Cut scrap paper into 80 'cards' and divide them into four equal piles. Take five minutes to brainstorm options for each pile – 20 characters, 20 locations, 20 objects and 20 proverbs/sayings (pick some from a book if you can't think of 20). Shuffle the piles and deal yourself one card from each pile. You now have four ingredients to make a story. For ten minutes, brainstorm your first thoughts about how they come together and what happens.

## ⑩ Ask questions

Ask questions and more questions to find your story. What are a young star's problems? Do they worry about their looks and develop an eating disorder? Do they long for a true friend? Do they want a different career? Asking questions will help you to see their story.

### Case study

Jack Gantos created the **Joey Pigza** trilogy after meeting children with Attention Deficit Hyperactivity Disorder on his schools visits. One night he was writing about a particular boy in his diary and the character of Joey Pigza started coming to life. Gantos was inspired to write a story to show that children whose lives are managed by 'meds' are not bad kids.

### ⑪ Research a setting

In realistic fiction, the setting will play a big part in how everyone behaves, be it a war zone or the city streets. To tell a convincing tale, you will need to understand how the setting operates.

### ⑫ Make the location thrilling

Don't bore readers by describing absolutely everything about your physical location. But make sure you know how the location will influence the human story. This calls for research. Imagine you're doing a geography assignment; look for details on human settlement patterns, climate, natural history, communications or emergency services. Sketching setting details will help you to understand them better. Choose the most dramatic features to use in your story.

### ⑬ Add more action

In Jack London's *White Fang*, he conjures the harshness of the terrain in this grizzly incident:

> *There were cries of men, the churn of sleds, the creaking of harnesses, and the eager whimpering of straining dogs. Four sleds pulled in from the riverbed to the camp among the trees. Half a dozen men were about the man who crouched in the centre of the dying fire. They were shaking and prodding him into consciousness...*
>
> *"Red she-wolf...Come in with the dogs at feedin' time...First she ate the dogfood...Then she ate the dogs... An' after that she ate Bill..."*
>
> Jack London, *White Fang*

## Case study

Jack London was heavily influenced by Charles Darwin's idea of the "survival of the fittest," an idea that emphasized competition in nature for the improvement of the species. **White Fang** displays London's view of the brutality of the natural world.

## Now it's your turn

### A sense of place

Go back to your 'chance concoctions' options (see page 18). Think about the 'character' and 'place' that you dealt from your cards. For ten minutes, write a scene that describes your chosen place from the character's point of view. Imagine they are upset (decide why first) and find ways to reflect this in your description. Take a break and then repeat the exercise, but this time write to reflect a positive feeling – joy, relief or hope.

## 14 Use the setting to reveal feelings

At the start of Sharon Creech's *Walk Two Moons*, Salamanca is shocked when her father insists they move from their Kentucky farm to live in a town. What does her description of her new home reveal about her feelings?

> *Tiny, squirt trees. Little birdhouses in a row – and one of those birdhouses was ours. No swimming hole, no barn, no cows, no chickens, no pigs...*
> *"Let's take a tour," my father said, rather too heartily.*
> *We walked through the tiny living room into the miniature kitchen and upstairs into...my pocket-sized bedroom...*
>
> Sharon Creech, *Walk Two Moons*

### TIPS AND TECHNIQUES

When setting any scene, think of ways to trigger the senses. How does it smell, feel, sound, taste and look from inside your own skin? Keep thinking too: how does it affect my characters and their actions?

## 15 Explore problems

Realistic-fiction writers mostly write
about human problems – being ill, losing a parent,
coping with emotions such as jealousy or being bullied,
for example. The focus is on how the
characters deal with tough problems,
rather than on location.

## 16 Use humour

Seeing the funny side of the worst situations is a real gift. Writers like Morris Gleitzman,
Jack Gantos, Sharon Creech and Jacqueline Wilson are masters at using humour when relating
sad events. They do not make light of issues by doing this, but present them in such an
entertaining or uplifting way that readers cannot put their books down.

## 17 Don't be too bleak

No one wants to read a book that makes them feel utterly miserable, so don't be too grim –
even if you are writing a war story. Aim to give readers hope that even life's worst tragedies
can be overcome.

# ⑱ Make a story frame

One way to make realistic stories extra special is to take an idea inspired by your story's main theme and weave it through the story like the chorus of a song. This isn't as complicated as it sounds. Here are some examples:

## Magic frame 1

*The Illustrated Mum* is about a mother's mental illness and its effect on her two daughters, Dolphin and Star. Jacqueline Wilson shows us Marigold's illness through her obsession with tattoos. There is humour as well as pathos. Each chapter relates to one of the tattoos, in this case a serpent:

*Marigold was knuckling her forehead, trying to ease a headache. Then she saw Star's empty bed and stopped dead, her arm still raised. She didn't say anything. She just lay down on Star's bed and started crying. These were new horrible heart-broken tears, as if she were choking. It sounded as if her serpent had coiled itself right round her neck.*

Jacqueline Wilson, *The Illustrated Mum*

## Magic frame 2

A stray dog creates the frame for Kate DiCamillo's *Because of Winn-Dixie*. It is about a girl who has lost her mother and whose preacher father is reclusive. The dog brings them and many other lonely people together:

*Winn-Dixie looked up at the preacher...wagged his tail and knocked some of the preacher's papers off the table. Then he sneezed and some more papers fluttered to the floor.*

*"What did you call this dog?" the preacher asked.*
*"Winn-Dixie," I whispered. I was afraid to say anything too loud. I could see that Winn-Dixie was having a good effect on the preacher. He was making him poke his head out of his shell.*

Kate Di Camillo, *Because of Winn-Dixie*

## HEROES

**Y**our hero is the lead actor in your story. You must care about them deeply and make readers care about them too. They must be as real as possible. Think of them as best friends or family. Or perhaps they are based on you?

### ❶ How to spot a hero

Writers find their leading characters in all sorts of ways in newspapers, on the beach, in a TV documentary or when some little thing triggers a memory of someone they once knew. The trick is to keep a lookout for them. Be ready to spot them.

### ❷ Add problems

Stories about people with totally happy lives are very boring. At the start of his tragic novel *Anna Karenina*, the famous Russian writer Leo Tolstoy says *'All happy families resemble one another, but each unhappy family is unhappy in its own way.'* In other words, readers are only interested in seeing how other people deal with their problems. The more challenges a character has to face, the more fascinating they are to read about.

### TIPS AND TECHNIQUES

Pretend you are your hero. Write their diary.

# ❸ Build the picture

Think what your hero looks like and what they like and dislike. What are they good at? What are their flaws and weaknesses? These can add more drama to your hero's dilemma. Now focus on their main problems. What is their history? What is happening now? Here, Joey Pigza describes what it's like to suffer from Attention Hyperactivity Deficit Disorder:

*At school they say I'm wired bad, or wired mad, or wired sad, or wired glad, depending on my mood and what teacher has ended up with me. But there is no doubt about it, I'm wired.*

*This year was no different. When I started out all the days there looked about the same. In the morning I'd be OK and follow along in class. But after lunch, when my meds had worn down, it was nothing but trouble for me.*

Jack Gantos, *Joey Pigza Swallowed The Key*

## Now it's your turn

### In their shoes

For ten minutes put on your hero's shoes. Think about their weaknesses – perhaps a wild imagination or a hot temper. Think of their good points too – a sense of humour, a caring nature or standing up for others. These could get them into trouble too.

## ❹ What kind of villain?

There may be human villains in realistic fiction, but often the main 'villain' may actually not be a person but the hero's bad situation – being on medication, a mother's mental illness or grieving for a lost parent.

## ❺ Bad guys

Just as in real life, there are people who behave very badly in realistic fiction. They won't be evil in the way that fantasy villains might be, but they can sometimes be terrifying. In *The Edge*, Danny has to face Chris Kane, his mother's violent partner. He loses control over the smallest things:

> *There was the time they hired a video without asking him. Chris stamped on the remote control until it was smashed to pieces.*
>
> Alan Gibbons, *The Edge*

## ❻ Misunderstandings

In Mark Haddon's *The Curious Incident of the Dog in the Night-time*, 15-year old Christopher decides to conduct his own murder investigation when he finds a neighbour's dog has been killed. The only problem is, Christopher suffers from Asperger's syndrome. Although he has a brilliant mathematical mind, he does not understand other human beings very well.

## ❼ Revenge

Bernard Ashley's *Little Soldier* tells the story of African boy-soldier Kaninda Bulumba. He has gone to war to take revenge on government forces for killing his family. But against his will he is rescued by the Red Cross and taken to live with a London family. At first, all he thinks of is escaping back to Africa to continue his fight.

## ❽ Victim of circumstance

In *Face* by the poet Benjamin Zephaniah, Martin has everything he wants and a lovely girlfriend, Natalie. Then there is a car crash. Martin wakes up in hospital with terrible burns. He has to learn to face his schoolmates' embarrassment and revulsion. And what will Natalie think of him now?

### TIPS AND TECHNIQUES

*Don't make your baddies all bad; sometimes they're just behaving badly, but do have a better side.*

## ❾ The rest of the cast

Even the loneliest hero must have supporting characters to interact with. Only through them do we learn what your hero is really like – by seeing how they treat friends, strangers, stray dogs or enemies.

## ❿ Good friends

The hero's close friends are likely to be drawn in detail. Find ways to make them interesting. In *Walk Two Moons*, Phoebe is an instant source of mystery for Salamanca:

> *I saw the face pressed up against an upstairs window next door. It was a girl's round face, and it looked afraid. I didn't know it then, but that face belonged to Phoebe Winterbottom, the girl who had a powerful imagination, who would become my friend, and who would have all those peculiar things happen to her.*
>
> *Phoebe was a quiet girl. She stayed mostly by herself and seemed quite shy. She had...huge, enormous sky-blue eyes.*
>
> Sharon Creech, *Walk Two Moons*

As we get to know Phoebe, we also find out that she makes surprising revelations, which no one quite believes. The function of Phoebe's story in *Walk Two Moons* is to bring us to the painful truth of Salamanca's own story. It deepens our understanding of what it is like when a mother leaves home.

## Now it's your turn

### Your hero's friend

Think about the main character you chose in chance concoctions. Who is their best friend likely to be? What are they called? How do they meet them? Are they someone older or the same age? What kind of relationship do they have? Maybe they started off on the wrong foot. Take ten minutes to brainstorm your first thoughts.

## ⑪ Silent partners

Sometimes the supporting characters aren't even alive, but they still do an important job of letting us hear the hero's thoughts. In Paula Danziger's *Amber Brown Sees Red*, we hear Amber telling her stuffed toy gorilla her worries about being split between her divorced parents:

> *The hairy ape still says nothing.*
>
> *I get mad at him. "You don't understand. There's only one of you. What am I going to do when I go to Dad's and I need to talk to you and you're here? I can't carry you back and forth, take you to school with me. It would look really dumb for me, a fourth grader, to take a dumb stuffed animal to school."*
>
> Paula Danziger, *Amber Brown Sees Red*

## TIPS AND TECHNIQUES

*Use scenes with supporting characters to show your hero's strengths and weaknesses. Show them losing their temper.*

# WHO'S SPEAKING?

**W**ho will tell your story – just one person or lots of characters? How much do you want your readers to know about all the characters?

## ❶ An all-seeing view

Traditional stories like Louisa M. Alcott's *Little Women* are written using the omniscient or 'all-seeing' view. The narrator describes all the characters and tells us what they think and feel. Here she describes the March sisters' reaction to the ending of their father's letter, which says that when he comes home from the war, he hopes to be 'prouder and fonder than ever of his little women':

> *Everyone sniffed when they came to that part; Jo wasn't ashamed of the great tear that dropped off the end of her nose, and Amy never minded the rumpling of her curls as she hid her face on her mother's shoulder.*
>
> Louisa M. Alcott, *Little Women*

## Now it's your turn

### Switching viewpoints

Write a short scene in which two or more characters do something exciting like climb a mountain. First write it from the omniscient viewpoint, describing what all the characters do and feel. Then write it in the third person, giving only your hero's viewpoint. Finally write it in the first person as if you are the hero.

*My life is not easy. I know I'm not poor. Nobody beats me. I have clothes to wear, my own room, a stereo, a T.V. and a push-button phone. Sometimes I feel guilty being so miserable, but middle-class kids have problems too.*

Paula Danziger, *The Cat Ate My Gymsuit*

## ❷ The first person

The first-person viewpoint (see extract above) – 'I did this, I felt that…' – is an exciting way to tell a story, but to be convincing you must know your character inside out. You can also use this viewpoint in letters, emails and diary entries to add variety and interest to third-person narratives.

## ❸ The third person

Another way to write a story is to tell it from the point of view (POV) of the main character. This is called the third-person viewpoint and is usually written in the past tense:

*It was the first block of flats Ben had been inside in his life…*

*His tears had dried on the train trip out to the grimy industrial suburb and had been replaced by an ice-cold determination to do what he was now doing.*

Morris Gleitzman,
*The Other Facts of Life*

# READY TO WRITE

**A**s your story starts simmering in your mind, it helps to write a few paragraphs about it. This is called a synopsis. It will keep you focused on your story's main theme and plot.

## ① Back cover inspiration

A good way to learn how to write a brilliant synopsis is to study the information or 'blurb' on the back of a book. See how it makes readers want to find out what happens next. It also gives the tone of the book – serious or humorous – without giving away the ending.

This is the blurb for *Out of the Ashes* by Michael Morpurgo, a story about the foot-and-mouth disease that swept across England in 2001 (right):

> *This is not a story at all. It all happened. On January 1st, 2001, Becky Morley begins to write her diary. By March 12th, her world has changed for ever...*
>
> Michael Morpurgo, *Out of the Ashes*

## ② Create a synopsis

Describing your story's main scenes can help with writing either a short story or a novel. Novelists may outline their chapters like this, in which case it is called a chapter synopsis. Mapping the plot in advance, keeps them on track once they start writing, although they may still make changes as they go along.

## Now it's your turn

### Write your blurb

Sum up your story in a single striking sentence. Then give a glimpse of the main character's problem and the plot in no more than three brief paragraphs.

## TIPS AND TECHNIQUES

*If you can't sum up your story as simply as the blurb extracts, it may be too complicated. Simplify it. As you work on your own synopsis and story map, ask yourself: 'Whose story is this and what scenes do I need to tell it?' Think about your theme, too. In realistic stories this is usually a human problem – illness, dealing with loss, bullying, family crises – and how the hero overcomes their difficulties to have a better life.*

FOOT & MOUTH DISEASE INFECTED AREA

## ❸ Make a story map

Now you have a synopsis that says what your story is about; a cast of characters; a setting; and you know from whose viewpoint you wish to tell the tale. A useful tool to help you with the next step in the writing process is a story map.

## ❹ Split into scenes

Before film-makers start filming, they map out the plot in a series of sketches called 'storyboards'. This helps them to work out how best to shoot each scene. You can do this for your story. Draw the main events in pictures and add a few notes to describe each scene.

## ⑤ Inspiration from a classic

John Steinbeck's *The Pearl* is a short realistic-fiction novel that tells the story of the discovery of a valuable pearl that brings nothing but misfortune to its discoverer. Here are the storyboard captions:

1. Kino and Juana's baby Coyotito is stung by a scorpion, but the local doctor won't treat him because Kino is too poor to pay;

2. Kino goes diving and finds a great pearl. Everyone is envious of his find;

3. On a pretext of treating the baby, the doctor comes and, learning where Kino keeps the pearl, later tries to steal it;

4. Kino goes to sell the pearl so he can have a better life, but local traders set out to cheat him. Kito decides to go to the city to sell it;

5. Kino is attacked in the night, and Juana tries to throw the pearl away;

6. Kino kills one of his attackers and the family flees

7. While camping in a mountain cave, three more men come and Kino tries to lead them away, intent on killing them;

8. Before he succeeds, one man fires his rifle at the cave, killing Coyotito;

9. Kino and Juana return, grief-stricken, to their village;

10. Seeing that the pearl has brought nothing but evil, Kino throws it into the ocean.

# ❻ Write a novel?

*The Pearl* is a short novel, but with its single storyline and two main characters, it could also work well as a much shorter story. Once you know your own story's main scenes, you can decide if there is scope to expand each one into a chapter and thus create a novel, or if a short story structure would work best for your narrative. Both forms may contain equally big ideas, but while a short story distils them into a few telling scenes, the novel elaborates and shows them off in different settings and circumstances.

# ❼ Or a short story...

If you choose the novel option (and they are often easier to write than a good short story), then try to think of each chapter as a mini-story inside a larger story. It will have a beginning, middle and end, but it will also carry the story forward. There will be much more space to develop both main and supporting characters and reveal them to readers in different moods and situations. There will also be more scope for building suspense with action scenes, plot twists and sub-plots. Dividing the story into chapters also helps to build suspense and draw readers in ever more deeply. Remember, a novel is not a short story made longer, but a short story made fatter.

## Now it's your turn

### Weave a story web

If you are struggling with your story map, try this exercise. Give yourself 20 minutes.
In the centre of a large piece of paper, draw your hero in a circle. Think about their problems. Then draw six spokes round your 'hero circle'. At the end of each spoke, write down something that the central image makes you think of. When you have six thoughts, work on them one by one. Extend each spoke and write down the next thought that comes to you. Work around all the spokes in this way. If there's room on the paper, extend the spokes to create a third set of thoughts. Take a break. Then run your eye over the web. Has it made your story clearer? If not, repeat the exercise with a minor character.
Keep looking for those story triggers.

## ❽ Great beginnings

You have planned your plot and are ready to start telling your own story. Focus on your hero. How will you make readers care about them?

## ❾ Hook your readers

The opening scene may show your hero's usual life just before a crisis strikes and makes things worse. Or you could dive straight into the crisis and backtrack later to explain the situation.

Mark Haddon's *The Curious Incident of the Dog in the Night-time* has a melodramatic opening:

> *It was seven minutes after midnight. The dog was lying on the grass in the middle of the lawn in front of Mrs Shears' house.*
> *Its eyes were closed...But the dog was not...asleep. The dog was dead. There was a garden fork sticking out of the dog.*
>
> Mark Haddon, *The Curious Incident of the Dog in the Night-time*

Here is the first puzzle – who killed the dog? But there is something unusual about the narrator, too. The detached, analytical way the scene is described is curious. What sort of person is the narrator? Now we are hooked on two fronts.

## TIPS AND TECHNIQUES

*Hook your readers with your first sentence and paragraph. Make your opening mysterious, dramatic or funny. Write it and rewrite it. Read it aloud.*

# ⑩ Create mystery

In *Absolutely Normal Chaos*, Sharon Creech begins with a letter. This is instantly enticing because most people secretly like the chance to read someone else's letters. By the fourth sentence there is also a mystery, and we guess, too, that the story is going to be amusing:

> 'Dear Mr Birkway,
>
> Here it is: my summer diary. As you can see, I got a little carried away. The problem is this, though. I don't want you to read it. I really mean it. I just wanted you to know I did it. I didn't want you to think I was one of those kids who says, "Oh yeah, I did it, but I lost it/my dog ate it/my little brother dropped it in the toilet." But please Pleeeassse Don't Read It! How was I to know that all this stuff was going to happen this summer?'
>
> Sharon Creech, *Absolutely Normal Chaos*

In Bali Rai's *(Un)arranged Marriage*, the author launches straight into the problem in the opening line. The scene is set for family conflict and a battle of identity:

> "No way! I'm not getting married."
> I was shouting, something that I didn't do often. My oldest brother, Ranjit, had provoked it... But then, after telling me a complete lie, he started banging on about how I would end up just like him. "One day, Manjit, you'll be like me. Married to a nice Punjabi girl, thinking about babies."
>
> Bali Rai, *(Un)arranged Marriage*

## ⑪ Increase the tension

It's all too easy for a story to sag after a good opening. Now is the time to turn up the tension. Think of your hero's problems. How can you make them worse? Stir and complicate!

## ⑫ False happy endings

Sometimes characters pick the wrong solution for their problems and find themselves worse off. In *Jessicah the Mountain Slayer*, motherless Jessicah runs away to the city in search of her father. But she struggles to survive on the city streets and to achieve her dream.

## ⑬ Add more threats

In *The Edge* by Alan Gibbons, Danny and Cathy escape from Chris Kane and find refuge with Danny's grandparents. But Chris Kane sets out to track them down, and Danny's grandfather has a racist dislike of Danny. And finally, there are the racist bullies at Danny's new school. All these threats intertwine and build towards a nail-biting climax.

## Now it's your turn

### Problems escalator...

Brainstorm your main character's problems AGAIN! First write their flaws or weaknesses at the top of the page. In the bottom left-hand corner start drawing a staircase. The bottom step will be your hero's problem at the story's start. Write it on the step. Draw a second step and write on it the next problem (make it a little bit worse). Repeat the process up the page for as long as you can. Keep glancing at your hero's flaws and weaknesses. Give yourself two minutes for each step and write only your first thoughts.

## ⓮ Add in the time factor

In *Walk Two Moon*, Salamanca goes on a car trip with her grandparents. They only have a week for their journey across America and mean to visit all the places that Salamanca's mother stopped at on an earlier trip (below). Salamanca is desperate to reach her mother's final destination in time for her birthday. On the last lap Grandma is bitten by a snake. Will they reach Lewiston in time?

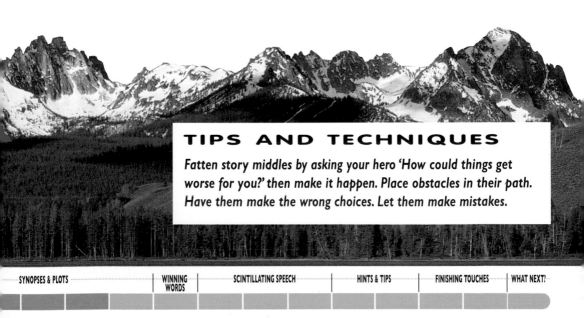

### TIPS AND TECHNIQUES

*Fatten story middles by asking your hero 'How could things get worse for you?' then make it happen. Place obstacles in their path. Have them make the wrong choices. Let them make mistakes.*

## ⓯ Dramatic climaxes

In the last part of your story, the hero's problems must reach a dramatic climax. After this the hero's problems will be solved, or at least changed for the better. Happy-ever-after endings should be avoided in realistic fiction. Instead, aim for an upbeat ending, where things work out hopefully rather than perfectly.

## ⓰ New beginnings

At the start of *The Edge*, Danny and Cathy escape by train from London to his grandparents' gloomy northern town. Danny has serious doubts that it is the promised land. But at the end of the book, when he repeats the journey and all his conflicts have been resolved, he has a different view:

> *He imagines the lowering mass of the Edge approaching through the late afternoon and feels a rush of exhilaration as powerful as in the last fifty metres of a race. He's looking forward to it, to freedom, to the promised land.*
>
> Alan Gibbons,
> *The Edge*

# ⓱ Heartbreaking endings

At the end of Jack London's *White Fang*, the wolf has recovered from his wounds and meets Collie's puppies – his own offspring:

## Bad endings

Bad endings are those that:

- Fizzle out because you've run out of ideas;

- Fail to show how the characters have changed;

- Are too grim and leave the readers with no hope.

*The other puppies came sprawling toward him, to Collie's great disgust; and he gravely permitted them to clamber and tumble over him…and he lay with half-shut, patient eyes drowsing in the sun.*

Jack London, *White Fang*

# MAKING WORDS WORK

**R**ealistic fiction needs sharp, vivid writing about how people behave. Every word must count! Pick the most telling details to bring your story to life.

## ❶ Use sharp focus

Keep descriptive passages short. Think of snapshot images. If possible make your description reveal something about the characters. In this example from *Walk Two Moons*, Sharon Creech shows us Salamanca's deep sense of loss:

> *Just over a year ago, my father plucked me up like a weed and took me and all our belongings (no, that is not true – he did not bring the chestnut tree or the willow or the maple or the hayloft...*
>
> Sharon Creech, *Walk Two Moons*

## ❷ Use vivid imagery

To help readers put on their characters' shoes, writers often use poetic comparisons or 'word pictures'. In *The Illustrated Mum*, Dolphin doesn't know how she will cope when Star leaves. She uses a striking metaphor to describe how empty she feels: 'a balloon girl with a trailing string lost in the emptiness of the sky.'

## Now it's your turn

### True words

Pick a word from one of your favourite books and see how many words of a similar meaning you can think of. You could also pick a new word from the dictionary every day to improve your word power. Find ways to use it – make a poem or limerick.

## ❸ Write from the heart

In *The Other Facts of Life*, Morris Gleitzman describes Ben's first experience of factory-farmed chickens:

> *These miserable creatures were from a different planet. He walked down an aisle, horrified. The lank, greasy feathers. The deformed beaks... And the deafening noise of misery.*
>
> Morris Gleitzman, *The Other Facts of Life*

## ❹ Heighten the action

Action scenes need crisp phrases that focus on what is happening. In *The Edge*, Danny and his mother escape from Chris Kane's flat (apartment). Notice the use of the present tense. What do you think it adds to the scene?

> *"Go!" says Mum. " We've got to go...now!"*
>
> *It's like the floor is tilting, the wall's closing in. Everything distorts...This is Chris's world, the terror zone. But there is no way back. They're running down the first flight of stairs. As they turn to descend to the ground floor they hear Chris's voice from the flat.*
>
> *"Cath! Cathy!"*
>
> Alan Gibbons, *The Edge*

## CREATING DIALOGUE

**D**ialogue lets readers 'hear' what your characters have to say in their own words. If well written, it brings them to life. Conversations between characters are also a good way to give information that pushes the story forward.

## ❯ The art of eavesdropping

The best way to learn how people talk is to eavesdrop. But don't simply listen for snippets of gossip. Pay attention to the actual words used. Tune in to conversations over lunch, in the street or on the bus. Look out for interesting expressions or particular patterns of speech. Watch people's body language, too. What do they do when they're telling someone a secret they promised to keep?

## Now it's your turn

### Breaking bad news

Your best friend urgently needs you on a mission.
But your parents say you can't go. Write the conversation as you break
the news to your friend. Do you end up falling out? Don't rely on tags
like 'yelled' or 'cried' to show the mood. Now revise it and take out any
unnecessary 'saids'. Cut down the words to the bare bones. This is the
essential skill of editing your own work!

## ❷ Following convention

The way dialogue is written follows certain
conventions or rules. It is usual to start
a new paragraph for every new speaker.
What they say is enclosed in single or double
inverted commas, followed by speech tags,
e.g. 'he said/she said', to indicate the speaker.
Speech tags may be left out if we know
who is speaking, or placed in the middle of
some speech lines to give the impression
of the pauses in real conversation.

The extract on the right is taken from
*Because of Winn-Dixie*, by Kate
DiCamillo. The author begins a
new paragraph for each new
speaker, making the extract
easy for the reader to follow.

*"Is it Halloween?" Otis asked
when I handed him the candy.
"No," I said. "Why?"
"Well, you're giving me candy."
"It's just a gift," I told him.
"For today."
"Oh," said Otis. He unwrapped
the Littmus Lozenge and put it in
his mouth. And after a minute
tears started rolling down his
face. "Thank you," he said.
"Do you like it?" I asked him.
He nodded his head. "It tastes
good, but it also tastes a little
bit like being in jail."*

Kate DiCamillo,
*Because of Winn-Dixie*

## TIPS AND TECHNIQUES

*Dialogue gives the impression of real speech;
it doesn't copy it word for word.*

### ❸ Study other realistic fiction writers

Listen to dialogue in realistic TV dramas. Read books by masters of the genre such as Ann Martin (left) so that you can get a grasp of what sounds convincing and what sounds contrived. This is not an easy skill to learn and will take time to master.

### ❹ Information through conversation

Conversations between characters can be used to push the story forward and quickly explain things about the speakers, the story or other characters.

### ❺ Let your characters speak

If you are writing from a limited viewpoint (third or first person), the only way you can reveal other character's opinions directly is by using dialogue. Even a first-person narrator may not reveal everything about their thoughts and feelings in the narrative. It is only when we hear them talking with others in dialogue that we learn more.

## TIPS AND TECHNIQUES

*Dialogue is never idle chit-chat. Whatever is said must advance the story. If it doesn't, cut it.*

## Now it's your turn

### Spilling the beans...

Write a conversation between your hero and a friend. The hero reveals something important – something they're ashamed of or angry about. The friend has to coax. Convey both characters' feelings. Find small ways to make them distinctive. Perhaps one has a pet expression?

In *The Illustrated Mum*, narrator Dolphin presents herself as a lonely, dreamy girl who often has to mother Marigold through her bad times. But at school, where she is used to being shunned and ridiculed by Kayleigh and Yvonne, we see a much tougher side:

> *"Her mum!" said Yvonne.*
>
> *They all sniggered. My fists clenched.*
>
> *"Did you see her tattoos?" said Kayleigh.*
>
> *"All over her! My mum says tattoos are dead common," said Yvonne.*
>
> *"Your mum's just jealous of my mum because she's a great fat lump like you," I said, and shoved her hard in her wobbly stomach.*
>
> *"Um, you punched her!" said Kayleigh.*
>
> *"Yeah, and I'll punch you too," I said, and I hit her hard, right on the chin.*
>
> *Then I marched out of the toilets, the other girls scattering in alarm.'*
>
> Jacqueline Wilson, *The Illustrated Mum*

## ❻ Find different ways of speaking

Dialogue may reveal the speakers' age, how well they have been educated and if they come from a particular place or culture. In other words, they will not all speak like you.

## ❼ Avoid slang

In realistic stories, it is tempting to use current modes of speech – 'pur-lease!', 'whatever!', 'babe!', 'it was like', etc. – as well as the latest slang words. Be careful. This will date your writing. It is better to use plain English, or suggest current slang by your own original use of words.

**TIPS AND TECHNIQUES**

*Watch out! Today's 'cool' words are tomorrow's has-beens.*

## Who's Who?

In the following examples, the dialogue reveals who the characters are and gives an insight into their personalities. This is all accomplished in the space of just a few sentences, as words are used sparingly and powerfully:

### ❽ Child vs parent

*"Where's Winn-Dixie?" I shouted. "I forgot about him. I was just thinking about the party and... I forgot about protecting him from the thunder." "Now, Opal," the preacher said, "he's probably right out in the yard, hiding underneath a chair. Come on, you and I will go look."*

Kate DiCamillo,
*Because of Winn-Dixie*

### ❾ Classmates

*"Yeh! People with babies have to be totally unhinged." It was Sajjid, as usual, who put the point over most coherently. "I mean, they stroll round all day with real ones tucked under their arms that keep bawling and messing and having to have their bums wiped—" "Not just their bums!" interrupted Henry..."Grotesque!"*

Anne Fine, *Flour Babies*

### ❿ Use accents

*"Might be the car-bust-er-ator," he said, "or maybe not." He tapped a few hoses. "Might be these dang snakes." "Oh, my," the woman said. "Snakes? In my engine?" Gramps waggled a hose. "This here is what I call a snake," he said.*

Sharon Creech,
*Walk Two Moons*

### ⓫ Non-native speakers

*"Who is letting you in? I will kick to them," he said. "My mum used to work here. I want to know where she went," I replied. "I know you, boy. You is polees...Please to get out or I kicks you."*

Farrukh Dhondy, *Run*

# BEATING WRITER'S BLOCK

**E**ven the best-known writers can find themselves stuck for words and ideas. They have writer's block. It can last for days, weeks or even longer. Here are some of the most common causes and cures.

## ❶ Get over your insecurities

It's your internal critic, the Story Saboteur, that tells you that everything you write is useless. Do NOT listen. Do some timed brainstorming instantly, e.g. the best meal/day you ever had. Write down just first, unedited thoughts.

## ❷ Find fresh ideas

Another cause for writer's block is thinking you have nothing to say. Again, if you write and exercise often, you will trigger ideas. You know how to search for them too – try the lost-and-found columns in your local newspaper. Or repeat any of the exercises in this book.

## Now it's your turn

### Positive thinking

Write a note to yourself in your writing notebook:

### 'WRITING IS MAGIC. BUT IT'S NOT ALWAYS EASY!'

Brainstorm for five minutes, listing all the things you find hard about writing. Now list all the things you love about writing. Look over the problems. Can they be fixed with more time, practice and reading? Is learning to write more important to you than the problems? If yes, your stories will get written!

# ❸ Coping with criticism

No one enjoys rejection or criticism, but it is an important part of learning to be a writer. If you ask someone to read your stories, be prepared for some negative comments. They may be more useful than flattery. Take the chance to improve and rewrite your story.

# ❹ Don't assume other writers are better than you

This is a common trap that even experienced writers fall into.

It is up to you how good a writer you become. The more you practise, the more you will improve. Read other writers' work to help you learn your craft. Be grateful for their guidance, but don't envy them. Remember! You may not become a successful novelist, but you could use your writing skills in other ways.

## TIPS AND TECHNIQUES

*To avoid writer's block:*
- *Keep reading.*
- *Always carry a notebook and write down anything interesting.*
- *Keep a diary and set yourself a daily word target, say 300 words.*
- *Deal yourself more options in chance concoctions.*
- *Watch an episode of your favourite TV show, then re-write it as a story.*
- *Give your conscious mind a break – tidy your room, walk the dog – you will find something to make a story.*
- *Do more reading...*

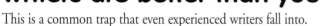

### ❺ Understanding writer's block

The kind of writer's block that leaves you stuck mid-story usually means that there has not been enough planning.

The important thing is don't panic!

### ❻ Shake up your thoughts

If your story has stalled, look at your synopsis again. Read it carefully. Have you wandered off the point and sent your hero up a 'blind alley' (left)? If so, put on your hero's shoes and ask: 'How am I feeling?' 'What's my next move?' Brainstorm for ten minutes.

### ❼ Try a group practice

Writing is a lonely occupation. Sometimes talking your ideas through can unblock an obstacle. Brainstorm with friends. Tell them the story so far. Then let them take turns to say what happens next.

## Now it's your turn

### Correspondence course

Make your hero your pen pal. Write them letters or emails. Write their replies to you. Compete with each other: who can tell the best anecdote? Maybe you are jealous over something your hero has or can do. Maybe you boast about something you can do to make up for this. Start building a REAL relationship. Who knows what brilliant ideas may emerge!

## ❽ Interrogate your characters

If your main character still isn't coming to life, write a brief description of them, then ask your friends to add their ideas. Give each person two minutes. Don't worry about complete sentences. Mull over the results. Have you learned something new about your character?

## ❾ Write a group story

Use the chance-concoctions cards to create a group story. Everyone takes a card – either a character, place, object or saying – and develops this element of the story. Sit in a circle and take it in turns to make suggestions. The end result will be something like a chapter synopsis, which you can develop later.

## TIPS AND TECHNIQUES

*Don't forget to play the 'what if?' game when stories stall.*
*What if my hero finds out that his father isn't his real father?*

# PREPARING YOUR WORK

**O**nce your finished story has been 'resting' for a few weeks, it is time to edit it. You will be able to see it with fresh eyes and spot any flaws more easily.

## ① Editing

Reading your work aloud will help you to simplify rambling sentences and clunky dialogue. Cut out all unnecessary adjectives and adverbs. Once you have cut down the number of words, decide how well the story works. Does it have a satisfying end? Has the hero resolved their problems? Now write it out afresh, or type it up on a computer.

This is your manuscript.

## ② Think of a title

It is important to think up a good title; choose something intriguing and eye catching. Think about some titles you know and like.

## ③ Be professional

Type the title on a title page, along with your name, address, telephone number and email address (repeat this information on the last page). Print the rest of your manuscript on one side of A4 white paper, with wide margins and double line spacing. Pages should be numbered, and new chapters should start on a new page. This is what you need to do if you are sending it to a publisher, magazine or agent. But if you are sharing a story with family and friends, give it an attractive cover too.

### TIPS AND TECHNIQUES

*Whether you type up your story on a computer or do it by hand, always make a copy before you give to anyone to read.*

# ❹ Make your own book

If your school has its own publishing lab, why not use it to 'publish' your own story or to make a class story anthology (collection). A computer will let you choose your own font (print style) and justify the text (making even length margins like a professionally printed page). When you have typed and saved your story to a file, you can edit it quickly with the spell- and grammar checker, or move sections of your story around using the 'cut and paste' facility, which saves a lot of rewriting. Having your story on a computer file also means you can print a copy whenever you need one, or revise the whole story if you want to.

## Case study

*Anne Fine writes all her stories in soft pencil that is easy to rub out. She ends up surrounded by rubbings. Even when she has finished a story, she does lots of revision and editing. It takes her about a year to write a children's book.*

## ❺ Some places to publish your story

The next step is to find an audience for your realistic-fiction work. Family members or classmates may be receptive. Or you may want to distribute your work via a publishing house or online site.

## ❻ Some places to publish your story

There are several magazines and a number of writing websites that accept stories and novel chapters from young writers. Some give writing advice. Several run regular competitions. Each site has its own rules about submitting work to them, so make sure you read them carefully before you send in a story. See page 62 for more details. You can also:

• Send stories to your school magazine. If your school doesn't have one, start your own with like-minded friends!

• Keep your eyes peeled when reading your local newspaper or magazines. They might be running a writing competition you could enter.

• Check with local museums and colleges. Some run creative-writing workshops during school holidays.

### Case study

*Sometimes struggling writers are writing the wrong thing! Megan McDonald, creator of Judy Moody, wanted to be a poet until her writing teacher told her to go home and rip up all her poems. He told her she was a prose writer. After looking up what 'prose' meant, she went on to prove him right!*

## ❼ Writing clubs

Starting a writing club or critique group and exchanging stories is a great way of getting your realistic-fiction story out there. It will also get you used to criticism from others, which will prove invaluable in learning how to write. Your local library might be kind enough to provide a forum for such a club.

## ❽ Finding a publisher

Secure any submission with a paperclip and always enclose a short letter (saying what you have sent) and a stamped, addressed envelope for the story's return. Study the market and find out which publishing houses are most likely to publish realistic fiction. Addresses of publishing houses and information about whether they accept submissions can be found in writers' handbooks. Bear in mind that manuscripts that haven't been asked for, or paid for by a publisher – unsolicited submissions – are rarely published.

## ❾ Writer's tip

If your story is rejected by an editor, don't despair! Every published book you have ever read will have been written over and over before it was accepted for publication. See it as a chance to make the story better and try again! And remember; having your work published is wonderful, but it is not the only thing. Being able to make up stories is a gift, so why not give yours to someone you love? Read it to a friend or relative. Tell it to your grandmother. Find your audience!

### TIPS AND TECHNIQUES

*READ, READ, READ,*
*WRITE, WRITE, WRITE.*

It's the only writing tip you will ever need.

# WHEN YOU'VE FINISHED YOUR STORY

**W**ell done! Finishing your first story, whether it is a short story or novel, is a brilliant achievement. You have set your imagination free and proved you can write!

## ① A new story

While you were writing the first story, did some new ideas start simmering in your mind? Did you make a note of them? If so, look them over, repeat some of the exercises to help develop your ideas and start a new story!

## ❷ How about a sequel?

When thinking about your next work, ask yourself: 'Is there more to tell about the characters I have created?' 'Can I write a sequel and develop the story?' This is what happened to Jack Gantos (right) and Joey Pigza. One book turned into three (a trilogy) as the writer explored Joey's problems in more ways. Sometimes a minor character might clamour to have their story told.

## ❸ How about a series?

Paula Danziger's *Amber Brown* is a good example of a character who keeps growing. One book simply wasn't big enough to include everything that happens to her. Each book about Amber is a complete story. But all the details of her life, her friends, her school and her parents' divorce carry on from book to book. You must really know and love your character to write a series.

## Case study

Megan McDonald developed the **Judy Moody** series by remembering her own growing up. She says that being the youngest of five girls often put her in a bad mood. When she recalls some moody moment it inspires a new story.

## ❹ Develop a character

If you have created a character who insists on having their own series, you need to think about whether they will grow up and change from book to book. Some readers like their heroes to stay exactly the same in each book. What do you think? Would this be appropriate for realistic fiction, or should your hero evolve from book to book?

**back story** – the history of people or events that happened before the actual story begins

**chapter synopsis** – an outline description saying briefly what is to happen in each chapter

**cliffhanger** – a nail-biting moment at the end of a chapter or just as the writer switches viewpoints

**dramatic irony** – the reader knows something the characters don't; it could be scary!

**editing** – removing all unnecessary words from your story and getting it in the best shape possible

**editor** – the person who works in a publishing house and finds new books to publish. They also advise authors on how to improve their storytelling by telling them what needs adding or removing

**first-person viewpoint** – a viewpoint that allows a single character to tell the story as if they have written it. The reader feels as if that character is talking directly to them, e.g. 'It was July when I left for Timbuctoo. Just the thought of going back there made my heart sing.'

**foreshadowing** – dropping hints of coming events or dangers that are essential to the outcome of the story

**genre** – a particular type of fiction. 'Fantasy', 'historical', 'adventure' and 'science fiction' are all examples of different genres

**internal critic** – the voice that constantly picks holes in your work and makes you want to give up

**list** – the list of book titles that a publisher has already published or is about to publish

**manuscript** – your story when it is written down, either typed or by hand

**metaphor** – a way of describing something by saying it *is* something else. 'The moon's a balloon' is a metaphor. It is a word picture. It tells us that the moon is full, not that it is actually a balloon.

**motivation** – the reason why a character does something

**narrative** – the telling of the story or sometimes the story itself

**omniscient viewpoint** – an 'all-seeing' viewpoint that shows the reader the thoughts and feelings of all the characters

**plagiarism** – copying someone else's work and passing it off as your own. It is a serious offence.

**plot** – the sequence of events that drives a story forwards; the problems that the hero must resolve

**point of view (POV)** – the eyes through which a story is told

**publisher** – a person or company who pays for an author's manuscript to be printed as a book and who distributes and sells that book

**sequel** – a story that carries an existing one forward

**simile** – a way of describing something by saying it is *like* something else, e.g. 'I ran like the wind.'

**synopsis** – a short summary that describes what a story is about and introduces the main characters

**theme** – the main idea that is explored in your story, e.g. bullying, running away, overcoming misfortune. A story can have more than one theme

**third-person viewpoint** – a viewpoint that describes the events of the story through a single character's eyes, e.g. 'Jem's heart leapt in his throat. Oh no! he thought. He'd been dreading this moment for months.'

**unsolicited submission** – a manuscript that is sent to a publisher without them asking for it

**writer's block** – the feeling that writers get when they think they can no longer write, or have used up all their ideas

Most well-known writers have their own websites. These will give you lots of information about the writers' own books and many will give you hints and advice about writing too. Try Jack Gantos at www.jackgantos.com and Morris Gleitzman's site www.morrisgleitzman.com.

The *Listen and Write* pages on the BBC website are all about writing poetry, but there are lots of fun exercises with rap, similes and freeform verse that will make your written words sparkle: www.bbc.co.uk/education/listenandwrite.

Ask for a subscription to magazines such as *Cricket* and *Cicada* for your birthday. They publish the very best in young people's short fiction and you can learn your craft and read great stories at the same time. *Cicada* also accepts submissions from its subscribers. See both magazines at www.cricketmag.com.

Make a good friend of your local librarian. They will direct you to useful sources of information that you might not have thought of. They will also know of any published authors scheduled to speak in your area.

Ask your teacher to invite a favourite author to speak at your school.

## Places to submit your stories

- The magazine *Stone Soup* accepts stories and artwork from 8- to 13-year-olds. Their website is www.stonesoup.com

- The *Young Writers Club* is an internet-based club where you can post your stories. Check it out at www.cs.bilkent.edu.tr/~david/derya/ywc.html

- *Potluck Children's Literary Magazine*: members.aol.com/potluckmagazine

- There are similar sites at www.kidauthors.com for 6-to-18-year-olds.

- www.kidpub.org/kidpub is a subscription club that posts 40,000 young people's stories 'from all over the planet'.

**Writing links** at Kids on the Net: kotn.ntu.ac.uk/create/index.cfm and Google Young Writers' Resource Directory: directory.google.com/Top/Arts/Writers_Resources/Young_Writers

## Realistic-fiction Books quoted or mentioned in the text

*Absolutely Normal Chaos,*
Sharon Creech, Harper Collins

*Amber Brown Sees Red,*
Paul  Danziger, Mammoth

*Anna Karenina,*
Leo Tolstoy, Oxford
University Press

*Because of Winn-Dixie,*
Kate Di Camillo, Walker Books

*The Cat Ate My Gymsuit,*
Paula Danziger, Putnam

*The Curious Incident of the Dog in the Night-time,*
Mark Haddon,
Random House

*The Secret Diary of
Adrian Mole,* aged
13 3/4
Sue Townsend, Penguin

*The Edge,*
Alan Gibbons, Orion Children's Books

*Flour Babies,*
Anne Fine, Puffin

*Great Expectations,*
Charles Dickens, Penguin

*Heartbeat,*
Sharon Creech, Bloomsbury

*Heroes,*
Robert Cormier, Hamish Hamilton

*Judy Moody* series,
Megan McDonald, Walker Books

*I Capture the Castle,*
Dodie Smith, Virago

*The Illustrated Mum,*
Jacqueline Wilson, Corgi Yearling

*Jessicah the Mountain Slayer,*
Tish Farrell, Zimbabwe Publishing House

*Joey Pigza Swallowed the Key,*
Jack Gantos, Corgi Yearling

*Little Women,*
Louisa M. Alcott,
Bancroft Classics

*The Other Facts of Life,*
Morris Gleitzman, Puffin

*Out of the Ashes,*
Michael Morpurgo, Macmillan

*Run,*
Farrukh Dhondy, Bloomsbury

*The Pearl,*
John Steinbeck, Penguin, 2000

*Un(arranged Marriage,*
Bali Rai, Random House

*Walk Two Moons,*
Sharon Creech, Macmillan

*White Fang,* Jack London, Parragon

Picture credits. Alamy: 10t, 18-19 all, 21 all, 34-35 all, 48 all. Corbis RF: 14-15 all, 16t, 17t, 22-23 all, 24-25 all, 32-33 all, 38 all, 44-45 all, 54 all, 62t. Creatas: 8 all, 9r, 12t, 20t, 26-27 all, 28-29 all, 46-47 all, 48-49c, 49r, 56-57 all, 58-59 all, 60. Fotosearch: 1, 3, 4, 6-7 all, 30 all, 36-37 all, 42-43 all, 50-51 all, 63b. Getty images: 52-53c, 53b. Rex Features: 5, 8-9c, 10c, 11, 12b, 17l, 20b, 30-31c, 52b, 55, 61. FLPA: 13, 39, 40-41b, 40t.